forfeit. The forfeits were things like 'Kiss the one love best' or 'Go to all the corners of the room, one, sing in another, cry in another and stand the other'. So it was a 'fun song'.

At the same time, the song was also being sung in other countries. In France it had a different name. Instead of being called 'The Twelve Days of Christmas' it was called 'The Gifts of the Year', and finding this out really set me thinking. I soon realised this is a wonderful love song. Any man who gave his lady all those presents just had to be in love with her. But I also discovered that the song was linked to the whole year, not just Christmas. It is a song about the sun and the moon and the seasons. I also noticed that in every single verse we sing about a tree.

Trees are very, very important for, if we look after them, they will look after us. They were growing here on the earth long before your, or my, great-great-great-great grandparents were born (in fact, before there was anyone living here at all) and they prepared the earth for us to live on by the way they make and give out oxygen for us to breathe.

You will also hear a lot about different birds in this song. If you read the old stories – the ones we call myths or legends – you will find lots of mentions of birds.

In the Bible, birds were very important, but I'll tell you about that later. Birds are used as messengers in legends, they are able to notice, and understand, the things which are happening to our environment (the world in which we live). In the myths, the gods and goddesses often changed themselves into birds, particularly into swans and geese, when they wanted to visit people on Earth. Sometimes when your mum tells you she knows something you've done and you can't understand how she found out, she'll say: 'A little bird told me.' Perhaps she's right!

As you read this book and learn about the gifts that were given on each of the days, try to count how many the lady received altogether. I think you'll be really surprised when I tell you the answer at the end of the book.

The First Day of Christmas

On the First Day of Christmas
My true-love sent to me
A partridge in a pear tree

In this song the most important present isn't even mentioned! Can you guess what it is? Well, I don't know what your answer is, but I'm sure the right answer to my question is love. Every time we give a present – a drawing done at school, a pretty flower picked from the garden or a present bought with our own money from a shop – we also give our love, the most important, precious gift that can be given in the whole, wide world.

'A partridge in a pear tree' is sung twelve times in this song and is very important. I've already told you a little bit about trees in our lives. In many places in Europe the pear tree was a special, sacred tree. So was the evergreen fir tree because it showed the continuation of life during the dark, winter months. This is why people took a fir tree into their houses and decorated it with bright objects, just as we have our Christmas trees today.

If you read the ancient stories which we call mythology you will come across the partridge. The Celtic people believed that it was a symbol, or sign, of Mother Earth, the earth from which springs all the good things of life.

In the traditional story of Adam and Eve in the Garden of Eden, Eve was said to have offered Adam an apple but, in researching this story, I have discovered that the 'apple' was more likely to have been a fruit called a quince. The quince was the first member of the pear family and is a close relation of the apple and of the rose.

There is a notice on a tree in a Spanish park which really makes us think about the importance of trees:

Ye who pass by and would raise your hand against me – hearken ere you harm me, I am the heart of your hearth on the cold, winter nights – the friendly shade screening you from the summer sun, and my fruits are refreshing draughts that quench your thirst as you journey on.

I am the beam which holds your house, the board of your table, the bed on which you lie and the timber with which you build your boat. I am the handle of your hoe, the door of your homestead, the wood of your cradle and the shell of your coffin; I have the sap of kindness and the flower of beauty.

Ye who listen to my prayer – harm me not.

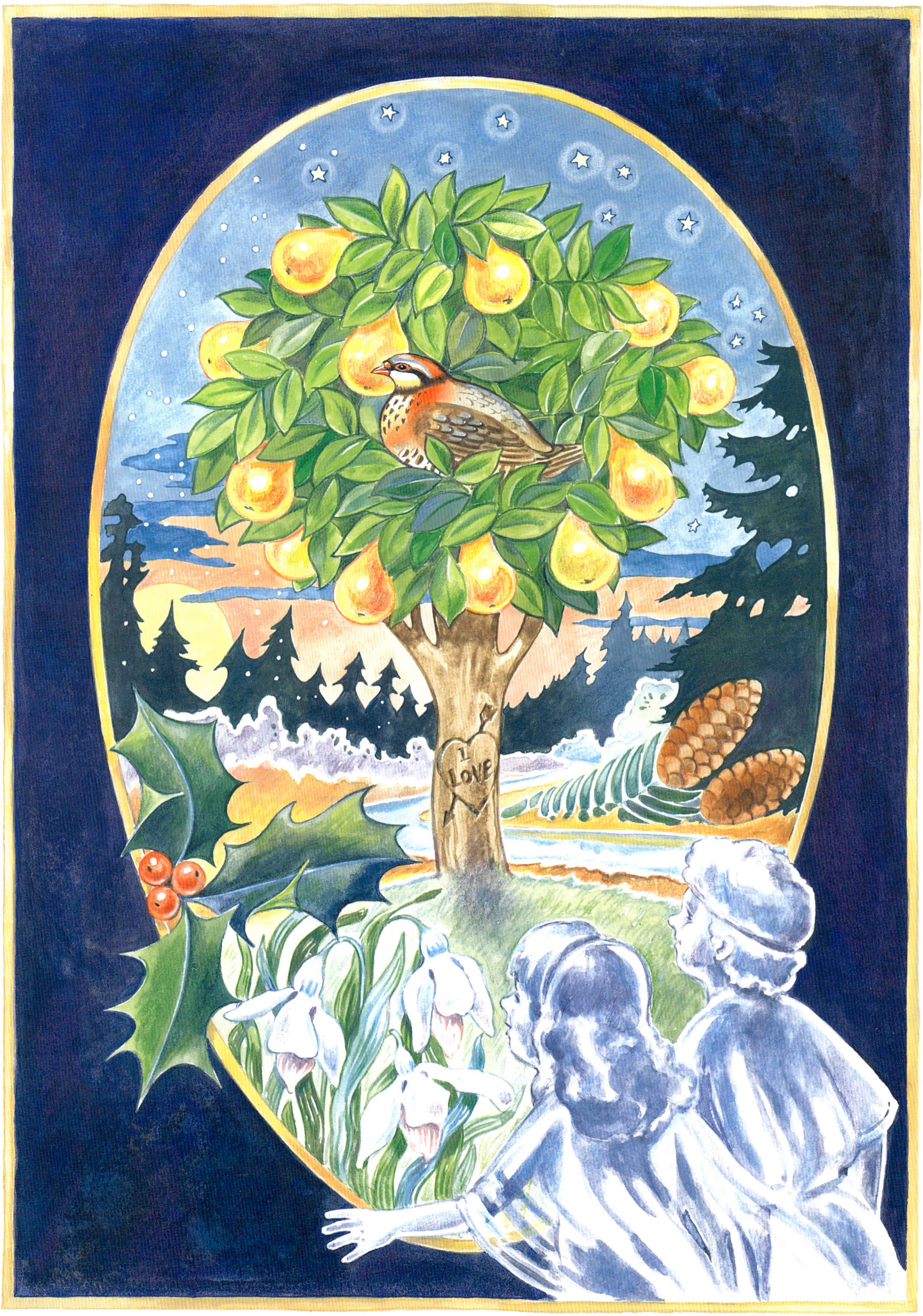
I
LOVE

The Second Day of Christmas

On the Second Day of Christmas
My true-love sent to me
Two turtle doves

If this song is about the whole year, then the first day represents January and the second day would then be February. This is the month when birds and animals start to pair up and build their nests and homes for their families. I expect you know that on 14 February we celebrate St Valentine's Day, when people in love send each other cards and presents. One of the most romantic gifts for a man to give to a lady is a red rose to show that he loves her.

The Prairie Indians believe the dove is a sign of rebirth.

The 'two turtle doves' are also a sign of true love. You might have heard the expression 'billing and cooing'. Doves do actually bill (which means stroking or kissing) and coo (which is their sweet, loving way of talking to each other), so we sometimes say that two people in love are 'billing and cooing'.

The dove is a sign of peace, marriage, love and friendship.

True love is associated with the moon. You may have heard people talk about being 'over the moon', which means they are feeling very happy. Usually when two people have just got married they have a holiday together, called a 'honeymoon'.

There are lots of other sayings connected to the moon. Do you know any of them or, if you don't, can you try to discover some yourself?

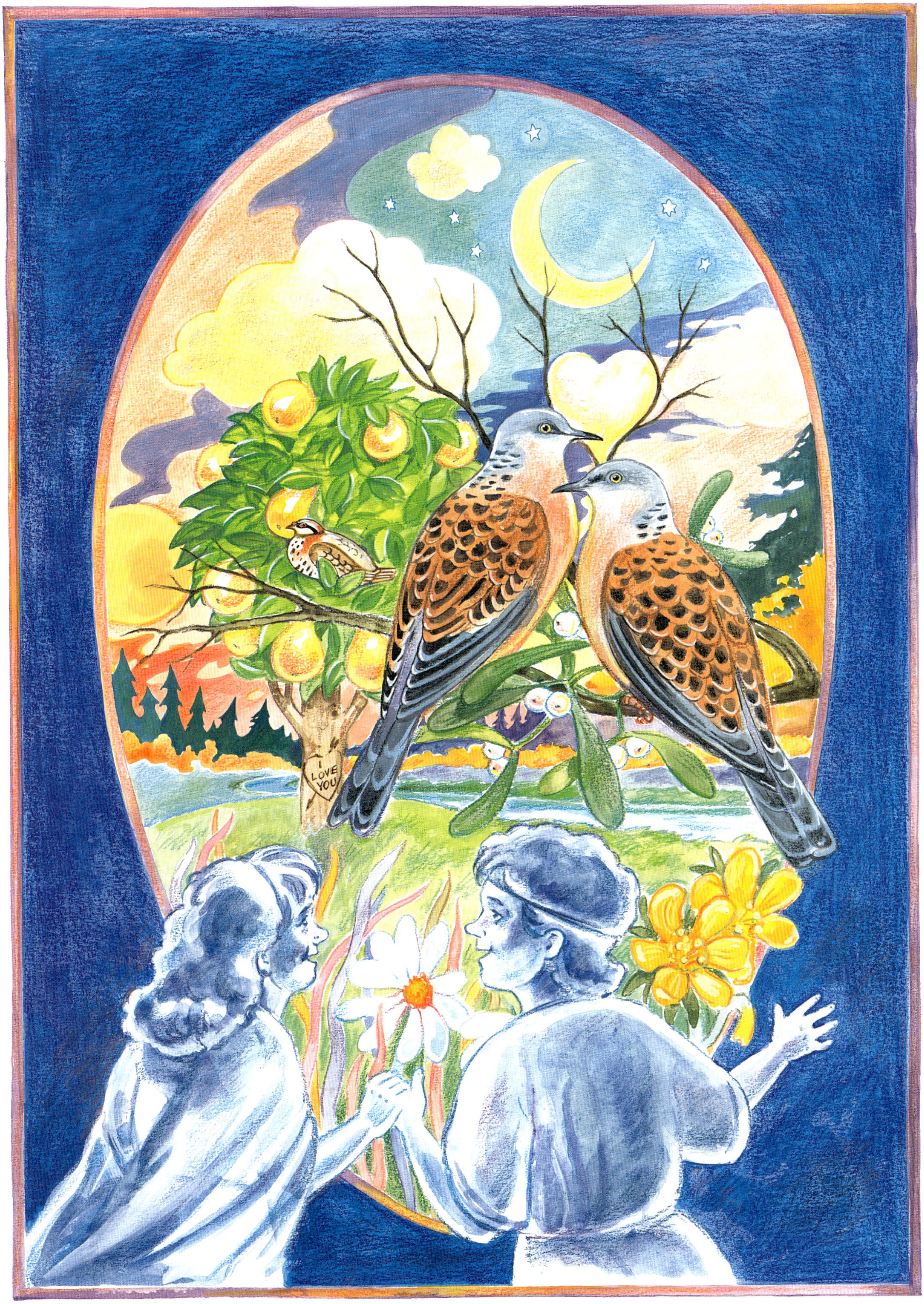
I LOVE YOU

The Third Day of Christmas

On the Third Day of Christmas
My true-love sent to me
Three French hens

The third day, or the month of March, is all about the new life that we see being created around us in the springtime.

The 'three French hens' with their beautifully coloured feathers are like birds of paradise.

The number three is very important – try thinking about all the things you know which 'come in threes'. Here are some of the ones I've thought about, and I expect you can think of a lot more:

The universe:	Earth, sea and sky
Time:	Past, present and future (or yesterday, today and tomorrow)
Cardinal virtues:	Faith, hope and charity
The Trinity:	Father, Son and Holy Spirit

In Greek mythology you can read about the Three Brothers who were the Lords of the Universe: Zeus was Lord of Heaven and Earth, Poseidon was Lord of the Sea, and Hades was Lord of the Underworld.

The tradition in Persia (now called Iran) is that there are Three Saviours, whose motto is 'Good thoughts, good words and good deeds'. Perhaps some of you have heard of the expression 'third time lucky'. Can you think of any more sayings about the number three?

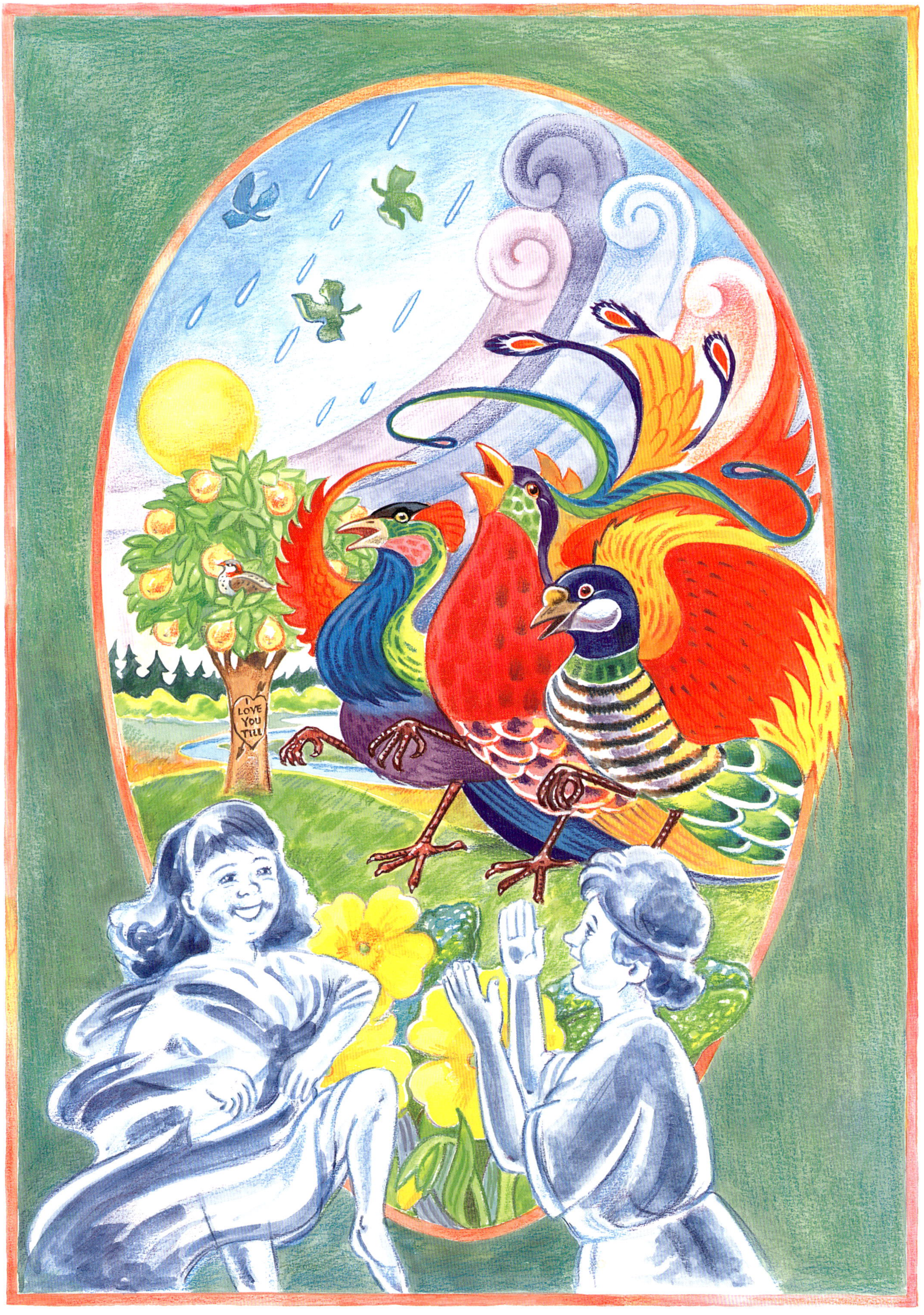
I LOVE YOU TILL

The Fourth Day of Christmas

On the Fourth Day of Christmas
My true-love sent to me
Four colly birds

When you've been singing this song I wonder if you've ever asked your mum or dad or your teacher 'What is a colly bird?' Sometimes we sing songs without ever questioning the meaning. I was curious about the word 'colly' and I've managed to find out quite a lot about it. In ancient Egypt the colliers were the charcoal-burners who brought warmth and light into other peoples' lives. Coal, colly, collier and colliery are all words of the same family. 'Colly' means black.

There are many birds which are black. I'm sure you could probably write a long list of the ones you know, but in this song I think the colly birds are ravens. The raven is a wise and clever bird and is also keen-sighted. It is written about in lots of stories. In the Bible, Noah sent out a raven after the Flood to see if the waters had gone down on the Earth. There is also a famous fable by Aesop about the cleverness of the raven. Do you know it?

The raven was important to just about every civilisation. In China it was the emblem of the emperor, a solar or sun-bird, with three feet which represented dawn, noon and dusk (or birth, life and death). To the ancient Greeks it was also a solar bird, sacred to their god Apollo. The Mayan people of Mexico believed that the raven was a representative of their god of thunder and lightning. If you ever read any of the Greek or Celtic stories you will find that when the gods wanted to send messages to one another or down to the Earth, they used the ravens as messengers.

Each morning the dawn is born out of the darkness of the night, black also represents the darkness before the very beginning of time.

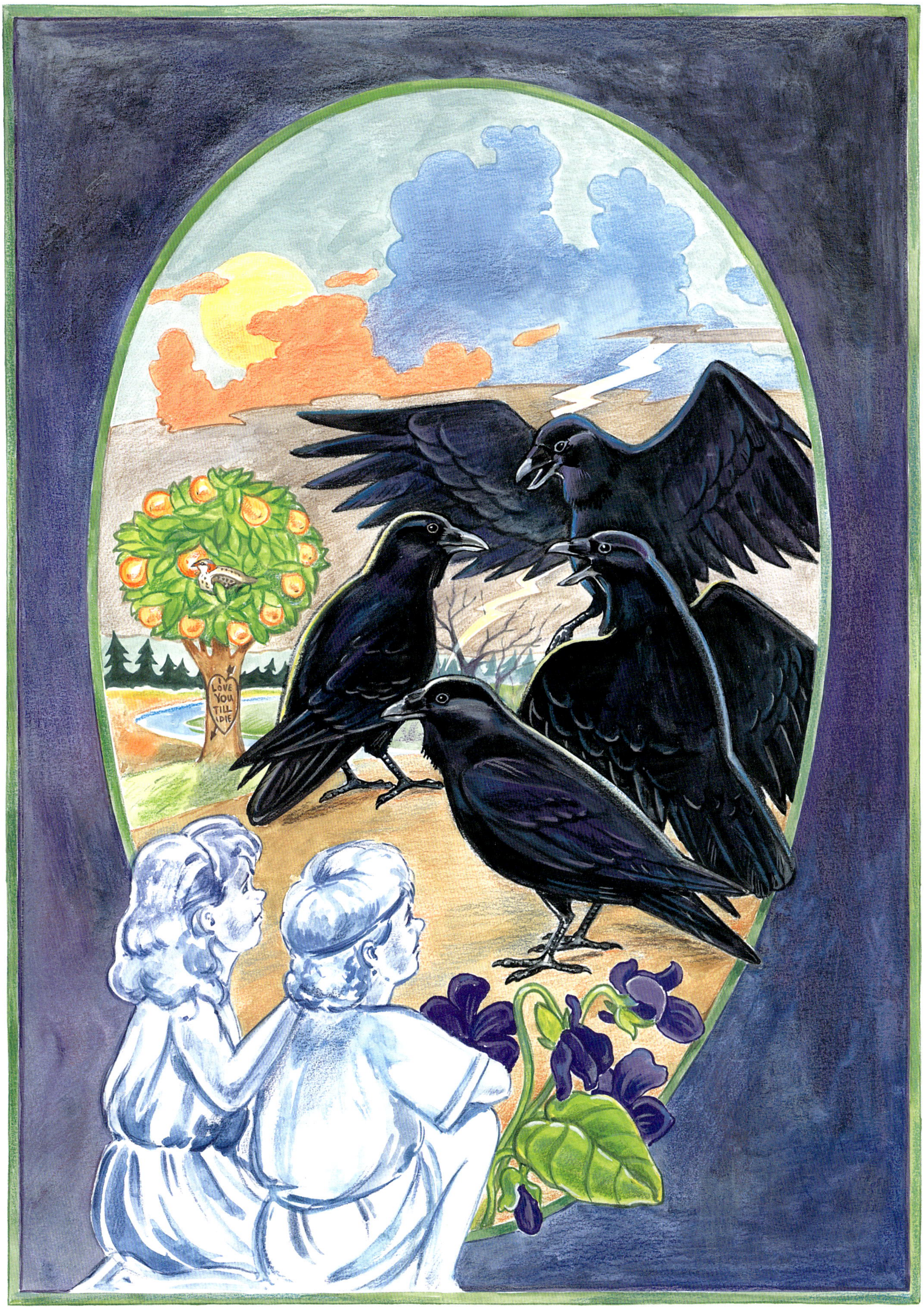
I LOVE YOU TILL I DIE

The Fifth Day of Christmas

On the Fifth Day of Christmas
My true-love sent to me
Five gold rings

If you really listen to the music when you're singing about the fifth day, you will hear that it gets a lot slower and more solemn, as though you've reached a really important part of the song. And I think this is exactly what you're meant to think. After the darkness of the fourth day with its black ravens, suddenly there is a burst of golden light.

Years ago, people singing this verse sang something quite different. They sang 'five gold spinks', which I suppose sounds a little bit like 'rings'. 'Spink' is a name used long ago by Celtic people to mean goldfinches. Gold rings and goldfinches are both signs of gold light. Goldfinches have both black and gold feathers on their wings. This makes them a good link between the dark fourth and bright fifth days – a sign that winter is past and the earth is reborn.

The five gold rings of the Olympic Games are related to the Greek god Zeus, whose home was on Mount Olympus. The Olympic Games are really a burst of energy and friendship between nations.

Gold rings are given as a sign of friendship and marriage. There are many games that are played in a ring as well as lots of circle dances. A circle has no beginning and no end. True love forms a never-ending circle. The giving of love and the acceptance of it are both as important as each other, after all, you can't give a present if there is no-one to take it from you.

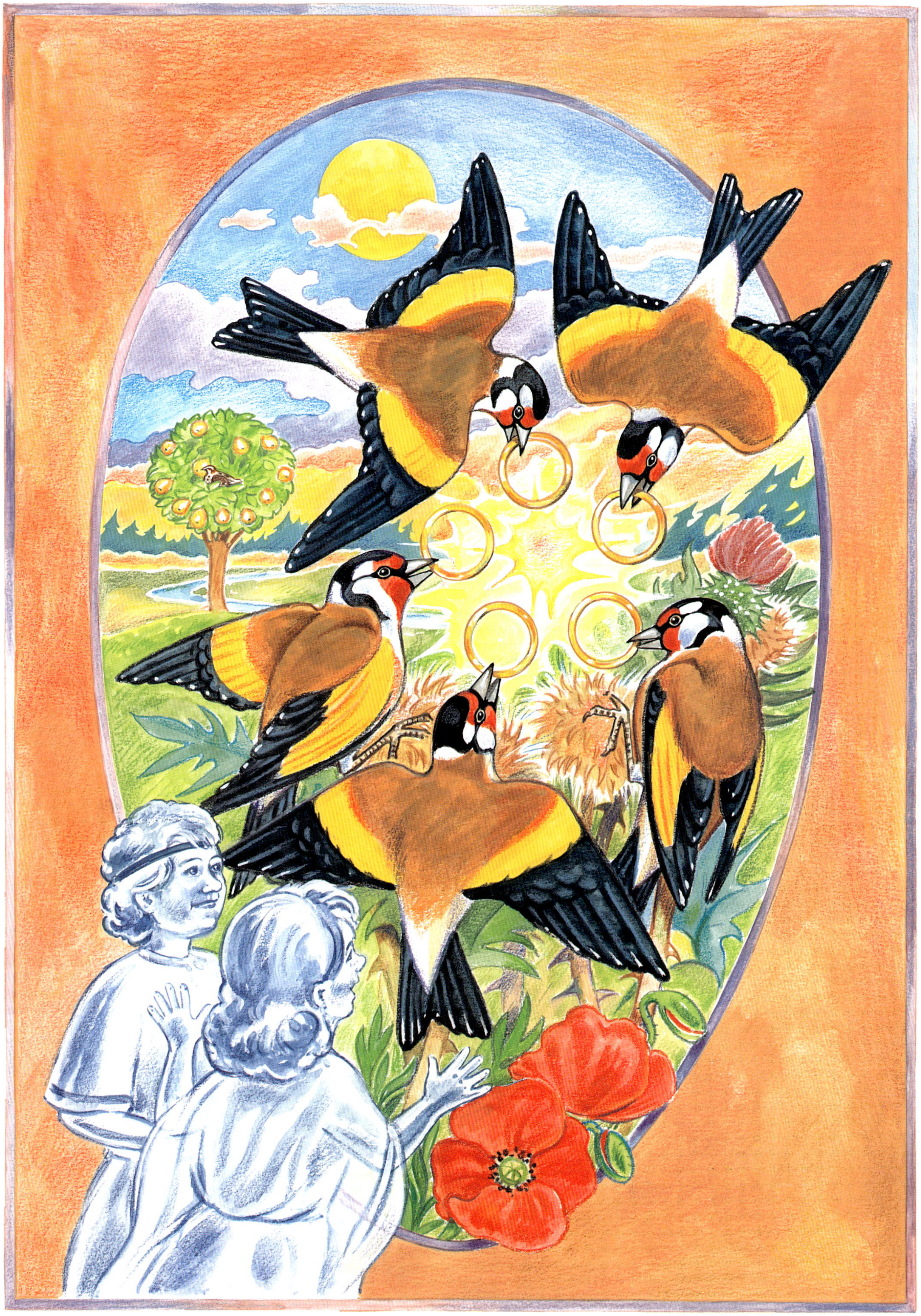

The Sixth Day of Christmas

On the Sixth Day of Christmas
My true-love sent to me
Six geese a-laying

The Golden Goose and her eggs are linked to the 'five gold rings'. In ancient times, the Egyptians, the Mayans and the Celts all believed that our world was hatched from an egg, laid by a goose. The Hindus believe that an egg rose to the surface of the water after the Flood and it was then incubated by a goose which gave birth to Heaven and Earth.

In the legends of Peru, the hero-creator asked his father, the sun, to make people to live on the earth. Three eggs were sent down to earth which were made of gold, silver and copper. In the story, nobles, ladies and peasants then sprang from the eggs and lived upon the earth.

People all over the world give eggs as presents. Some of these eggs are made of wood or china and are beautifully decorated, others are made of chocolate, and some are simply hen or goose eggs for our food. Eggs are a wonderful sign of new life. If you ever are lucky enough to actually watch a chicken or a gosling hatching out of an egg, you will understand what I mean.

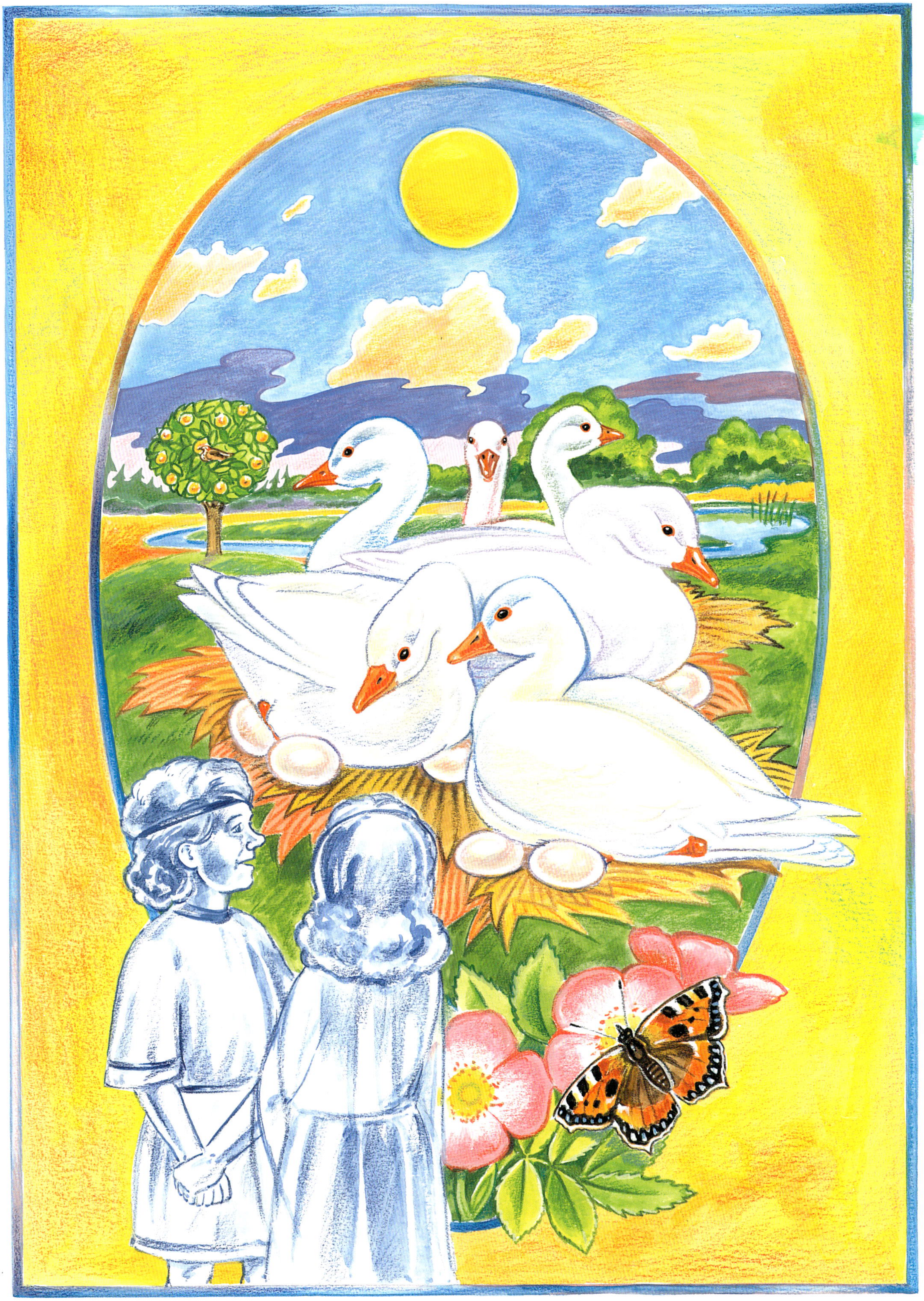

The Seventh Day of Christmas

On the Seventh Day of Christmas
My true-love sent to me
Seven swans a-swimming

Seven is supposed to be a lucky number. It is especially lucky if you see seven swans flying or swimming.

There are seven days in the week and seven colours in the rainbow. Do you know what they are? People called astrologers talk and write about the seven main planets. God, when He made the Earth, worked for six days and rested on the seventh. This makes the seventh day a very special day.

Chinese people hold their festivals on the seventh day. The ancient Greeks told stories of how their god Apollo, the son of Leda and Zeus, was born on a seventh day when seven swans flew seven times round the island of Delos. (This was after Zeus had turned himself into a swan to meet Leda, who had turned herself into a goose!)

So you can see that many people throughout the ages and all over the world call seven a lucky number. In Britain some people believe that if you are the seventh child in a family and your mum or dad was also the seventh child in her or his family, then it makes you a special kind of person with magic powers. I wonder if it's true?

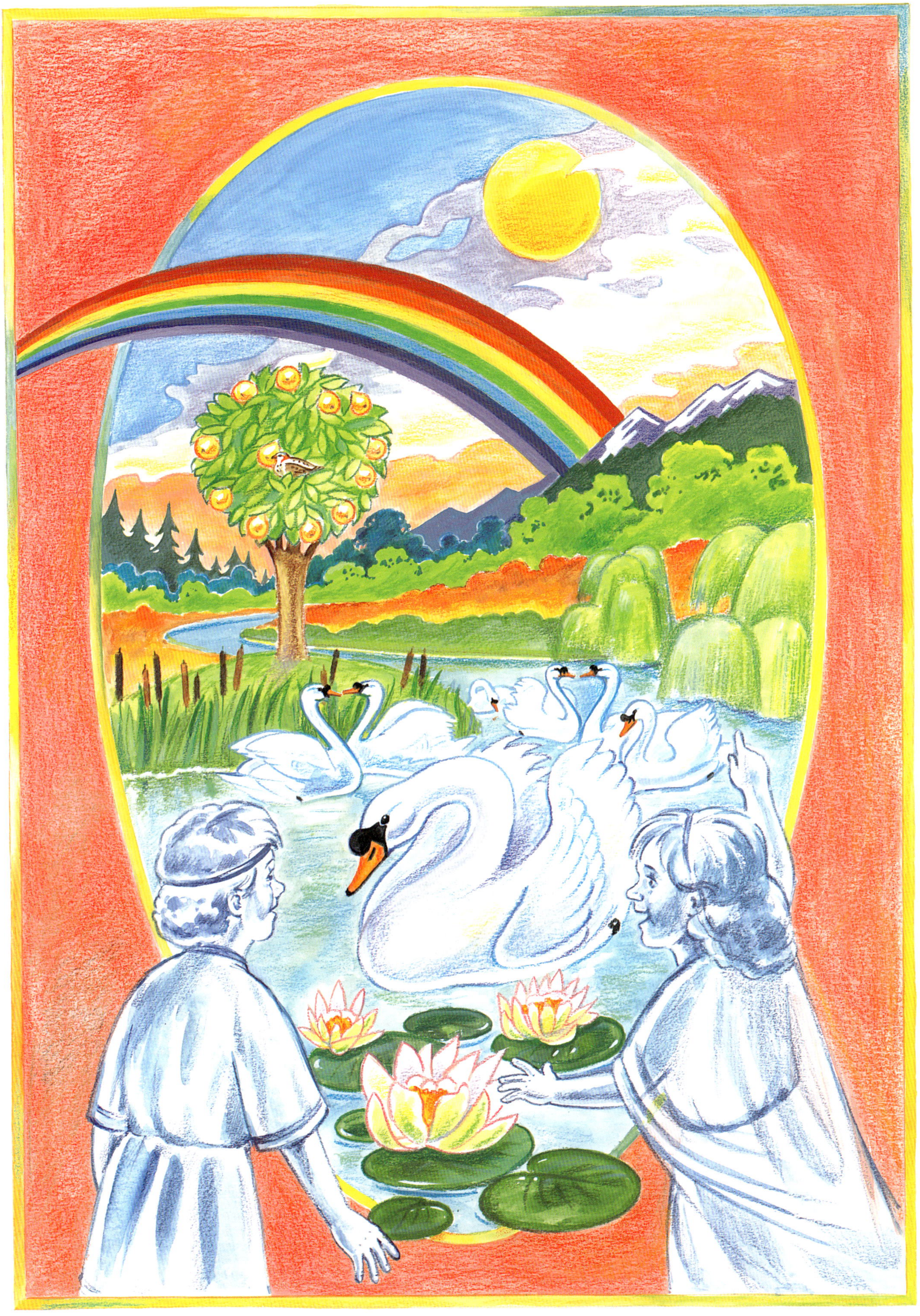

The Eighth Day of Christmas

On the Eighth Day of Christmas
My true-love sent to me
Eight maids a-milking

Milk is a symbol of life and knowledge, and you can read about it being a sign of rebirth in Egyptian stories. In the myths of India, life on Earth was born from a sea of milk.

When a baby is born, milk is its first food, without milk the baby could not live and grow. If you watch a baby animal sucking milk from its mother, you will see that as well as a food to make it grow, the lamb or the calf, the kitten or the puppy also gets a happy and a safe feeling. When a mother feeds a baby that is crying or upset or frightened, the baby quickly becomes calm and contented again. Next time you are in the countryside, watch what happens to the lambs and sheep in a field when a noisy lorry or tractor passes by.

A long time ago, in England at Christmas-time, milkmaids used to dress in their best dresses and dance through the streets, carrying milk pails decorated with flowers on their heads. They danced to tunes played on fiddles and they asked for a gift of money from the people who had bought milk from them during the year.

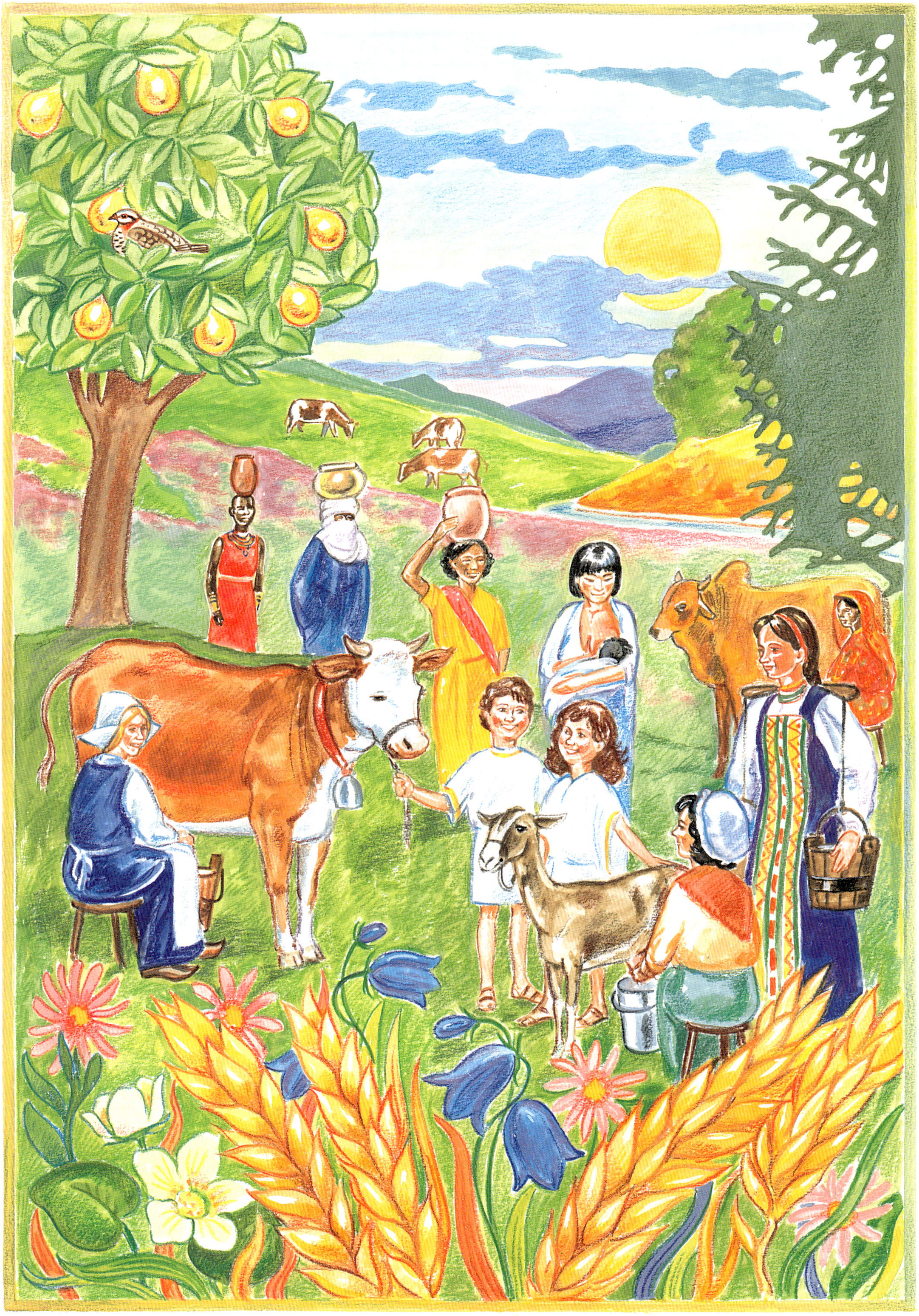

The Ninth Day of Christmas

On the Ninth Day of Christmas
My true-love sent to me
Nine drummers drumming

Long before people played recorders and clarinets, violins or cellos I wonder if you can guess what instruments they played? I can give you a clue, if you like. Perhaps you've got a baby brother or sister, or you know a baby next door. When the baby is sitting in its high chair, waiting for its dinner, what does it do?

I can tell you that the baby will bang on its chair or table and – you've guessed it – start to play a drum! I think you'll agree with me that the first instrument in the world was almost certainly a drum.

If you had nine drummers drumming they would create a vibration. Everything in the whole universe has its own vibration or rhythm. We each have our own 'drumbeat' inside us; it is called our heart. The heart is also another sign that is used to mean love. (Do you remember those Valentine cards?)

People all over the world have always sent messages to each other by using drumbeats. In ancient China the beat of a drum was also linked with the passage of the sun across the sky. The drumbeat is also connected with thunder.

Can you think of any countries where drums are used to send messages across the land?

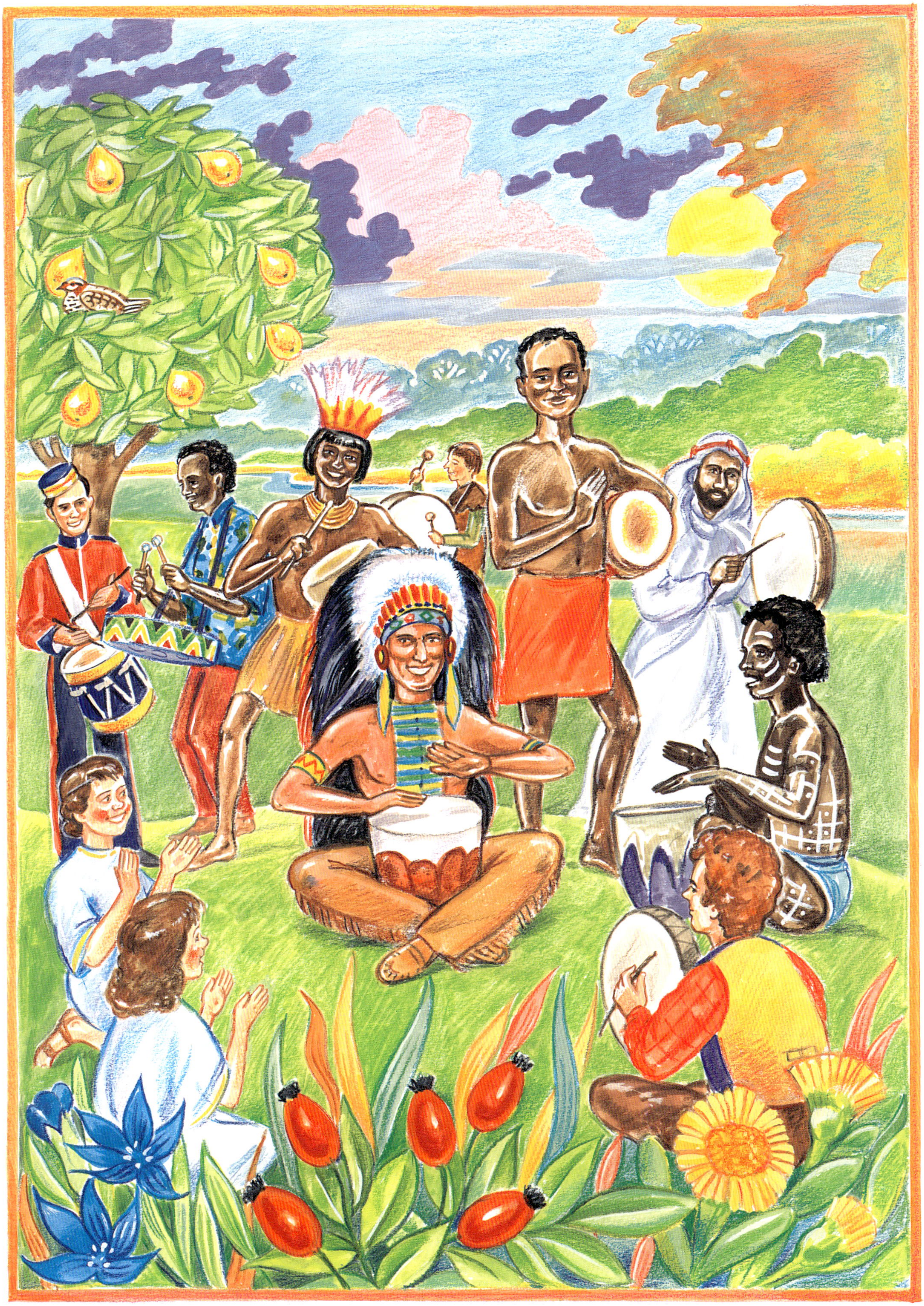

The Tenth Day of Christmas

On the Tenth Day of Christmas
My true-love sent to me
Ten pipers piping

For thousands of years, as well as using drums, people have made music by using simple, natural materials like canes and reeds. Have you ever picked a blade of grass and held it tightly between your thumbs so that you could blow across it? If you never have, try it soon because you'll be really surprised at the loud and quite different noises you can make by using just a simple blade of grass.

You may have heard music played on pan-pipes. In the legend or story, Pan was the god who invented the first wind instrument. He was in love with a lady called Syrinx, but she ran away from him through the forest. When she reached the edge of the River Ladon and couldn't run any further, she asked the river nymphs to save her. When Pan thought he had caught up with her, all he found was a handful of marsh reeds. Then he heard the wind blowing through the reeds and thought it sounded like a strange, sad music. So Pan cut some reeds of different lengths and fastened them together with wax, making the very first pan-pipes.

Can you see how a pipe is like the number ten? The upright stem is like a figure '1', and if you look along the circular bore it is like a '0'.

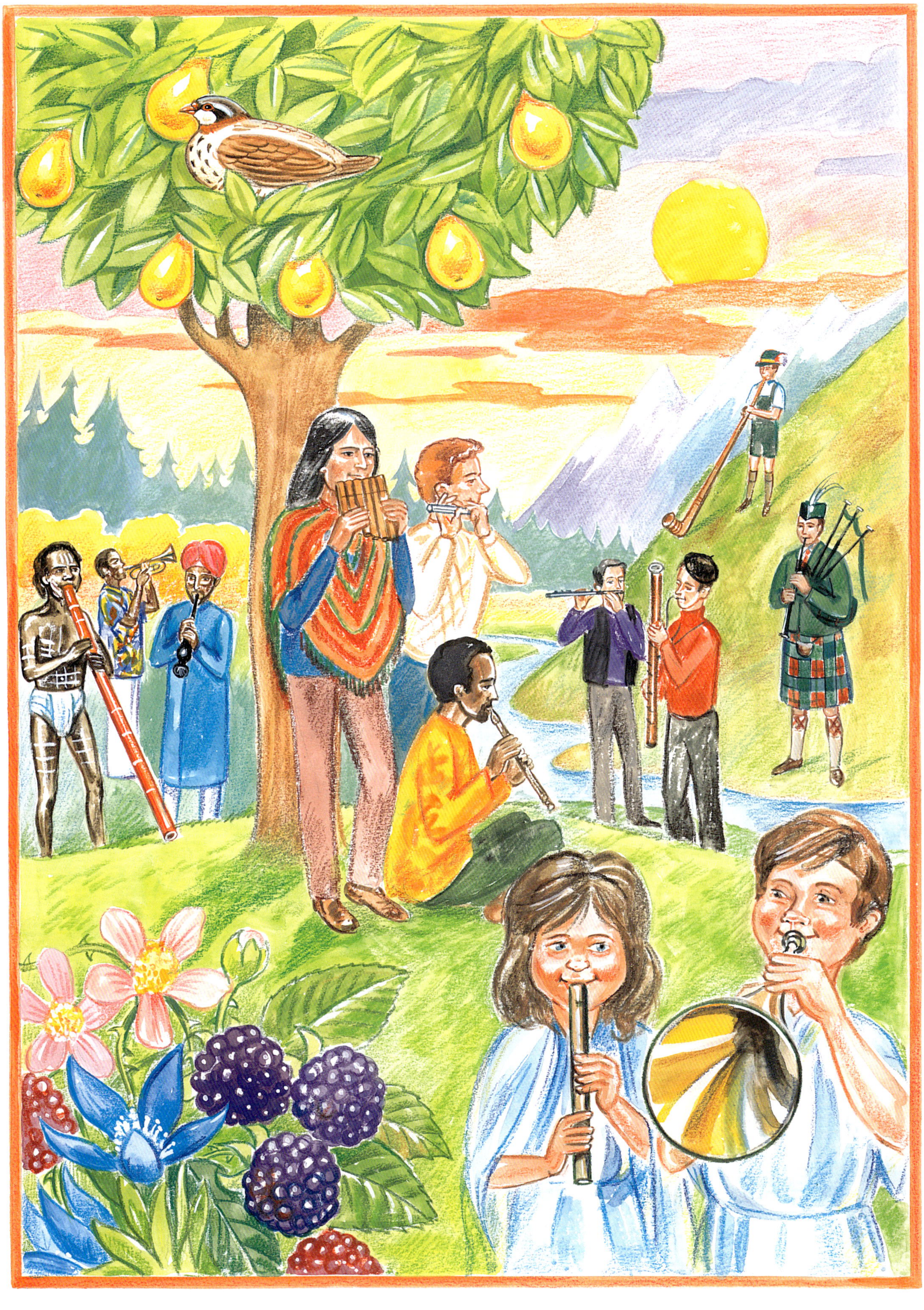

The Eleventh Day of Christmas

On the Eleventh Day of Christmas
My true-love sent to me
Eleven ladies dancing

People throughout the ages have danced on every possible occasion: to celebrate marriages and births, for hunting, war and feasting, to make crops grow, and to make sick people better, in fact, for every reason under the sun, or moon.

I am sure there have been times when you have felt so happy that you just couldn't stop yourself from jumping and leaping about, doing your own dance of joy. Dance is the rhythm of our lives.

Dancing is mesmerising and magical. In ancient times, dancing was an important part of the ceremonies that welcomed the springtime. Even today there are a lot of places in Britain where children dance around a maypole on May Day, weaving beautiful patterns around the pole with the brightly coloured ribbons which they each hold in their hands.

In ancient Greece the young men danced a special dance, called the Dance of the Kouroi, to welcome the spring and to encourage the crops to grow well.

Dancing has always been connected with the sowing of seeds. In ancient Rome there were special priests who went through the city at the sowing seasons (in March and October) dancing, leaping, singing and clashing their spears against their shields.

Perhaps you have heard of the Helston Floral (or Furry) Dance which the people of Helston in Cornwall perform every year on 8 May. Then the whole town becomes alive with colour, music and dancing. The local band plays for the entire day, and first the children, then all the adults join in the dance, even dancing in and out of their houses.

I think there is also something magical about *eleven* ladies dancing. If you've ever shown your friends a magic trick I bet you've said 'abracadabra' to make it work! This is an eleven-lettered magic word, and you can arrange the letters in a special way so that it looks like this:

```
A B R A C A D A B R A
A B R A C A D A B R
A B R A C A D A B
A B R A C A D A
A B R A C A D
A B R A C A
A B R A C
A B R A
A B R
A B
A
```

The narrow spout of the triangle is like the lines of force of a mighty whirlwind, just as some dancers whirl, getting faster and faster until you can only see spinning colours.

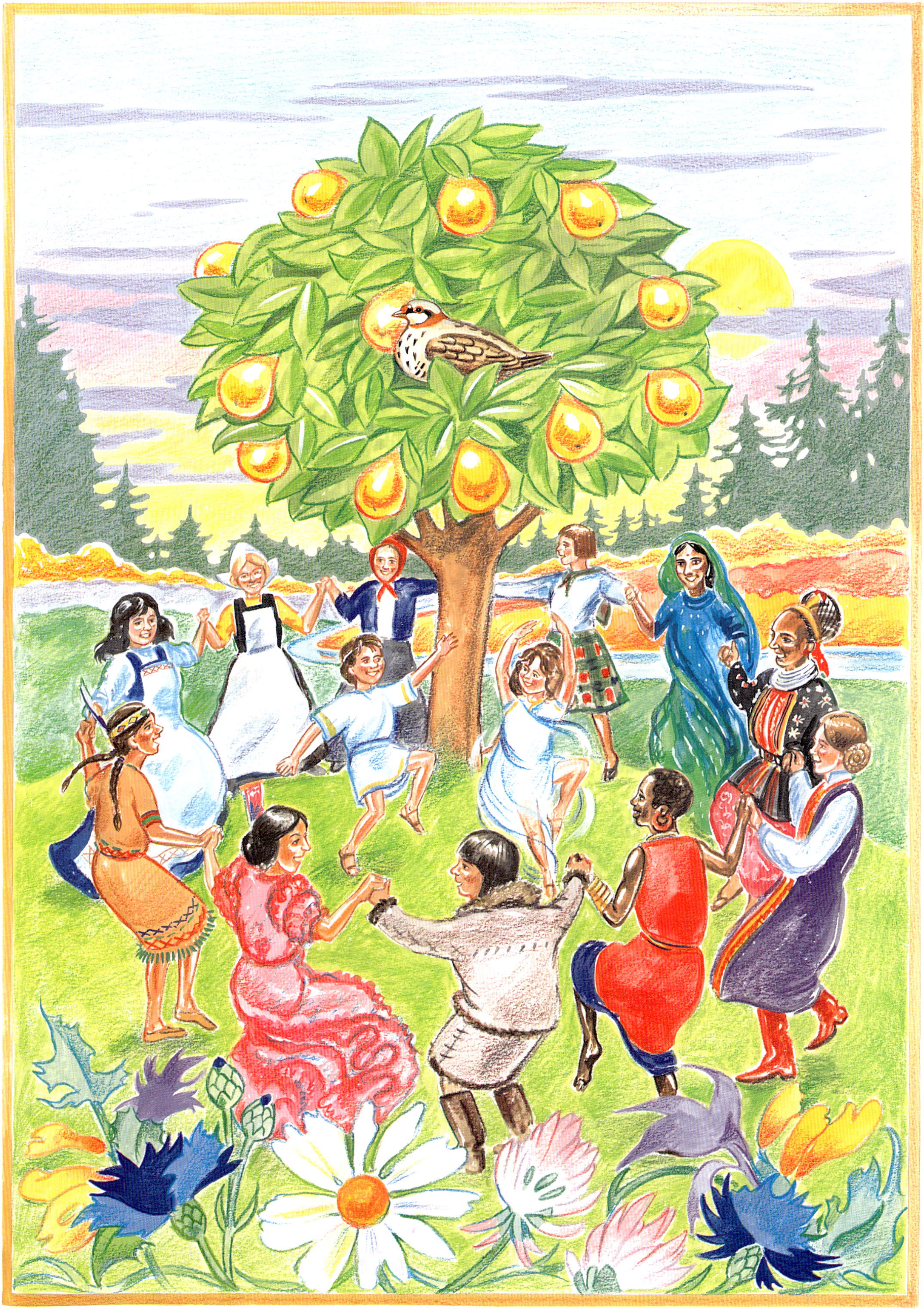

The Twelfth Day of Christmas

On the Twelfth Day of Christmas
My true-love sent to me
Twelve lords a-leaping

Did you realise that the 'Twelve lords a-leaping' are playing leapfrog? I expect you know how to play it, but you might be surprised to learn that there are more than eighty different ways to play the game! The games that we play as children are all part of growing up and help us to react correctly and get on with each other in a sociable, playful and friendly way.

Lots of playground games, and the actions which go with them, are connected to the seasons of the year and their activities. The game 'Oats and beans and barley grow' imitates the action of sowing seeds. There is a French game, L'avoine, meaning 'oats', where one child is the farmer and sows the seeds, then rests a little, and ends by leaping up in the air!

On Twelfth Night (the Feast of the Epiphany on 6 January) we still carry out lots of ancient customs. One of the reasons for the parties and the fun at this time of the year is to cheer us all up during the short days, when there isn't much sunshine. Years ago, when most people grew their own food for their families and their animals, December and January were difficult months because the ground was too hard to dig. So, many of the Christmas celebrations were not just to cheer everyone up and while away the winter, but also to invite the sun to shine again and welcome back the spring.

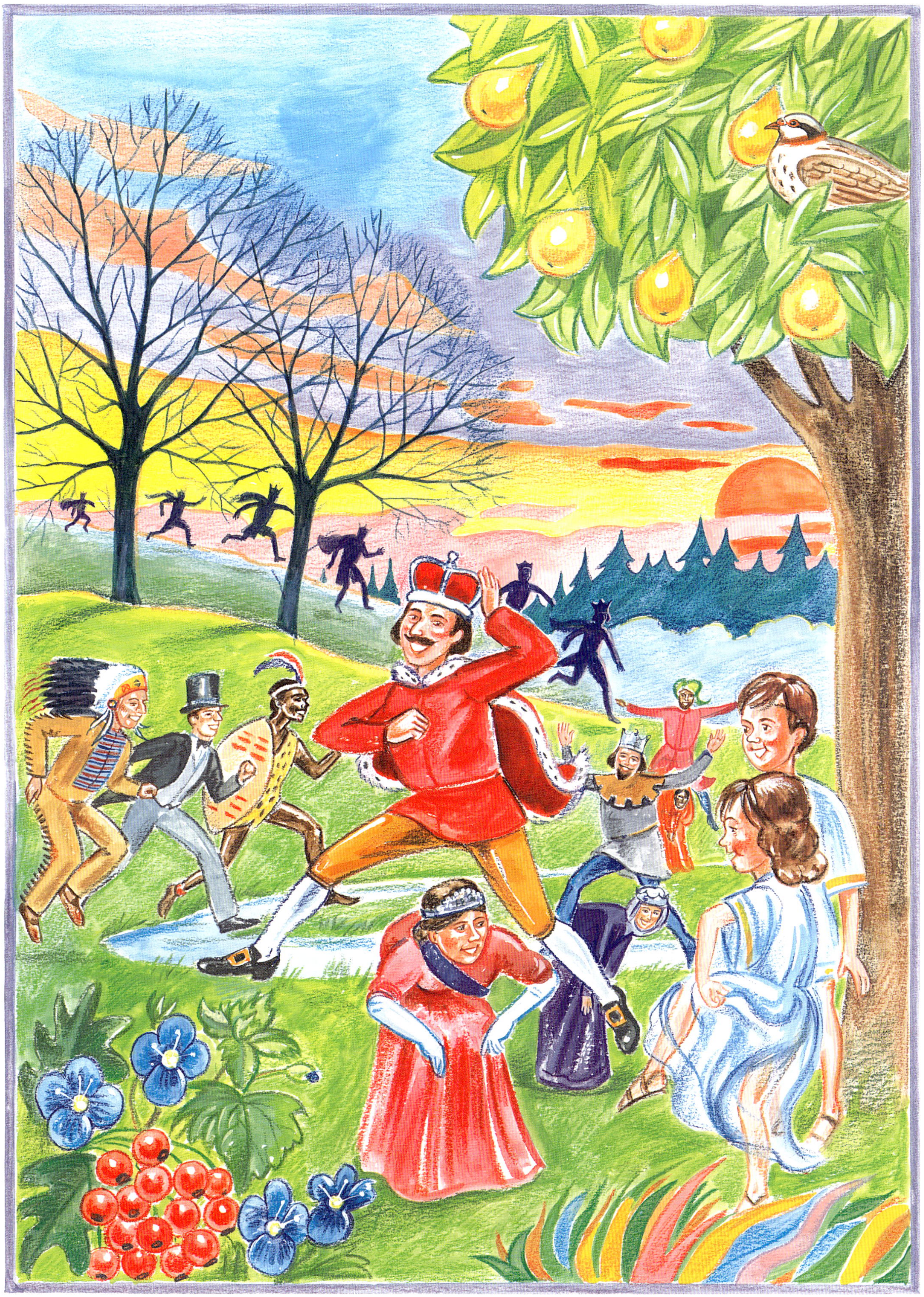

12 Days of Christmas

Two turtle doves And a partridge in a pear tree. 4. On the fourth day of Christmas My true-love sent to me Four col-ly birds, Three French hens, Two turtle doves And a partridge in a pear tree. 5. On the fifth day of Christmas My true-love sent to me Five gold rings, Four colly birds, Three French hens, Two turtle doves And a partridge in a pear tree. 6. On the

sixth day of Christmas my true-love sent to me	Six geese a-laying,
seventh day	Seven swans a-swimming, *(to 6)*
eighth day	Eight maids a-milking, *(to 7)*
ninth day	Nine drummers drumming, *(to 8)*
tenth day	Ten pipers piping, *(to 9)*
eleventh day	E-lev-en ladies dancing, *(to 10)*
twelfth day	Twelve lords a-leaping, *(to 11)*

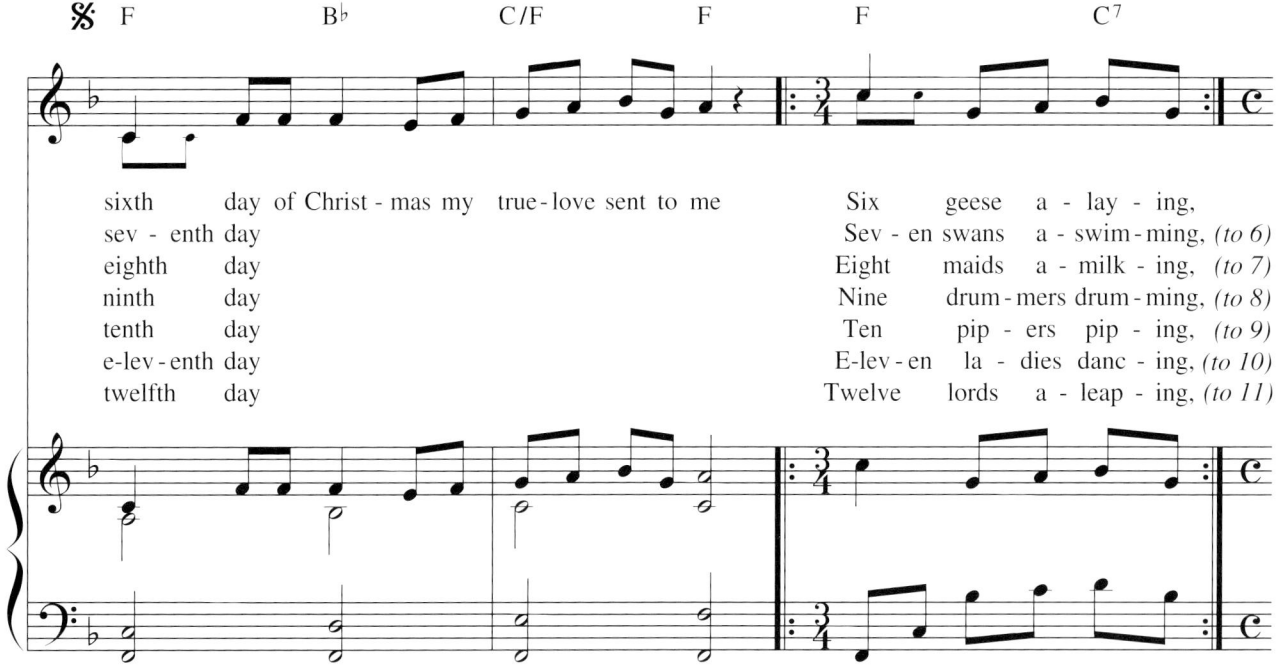

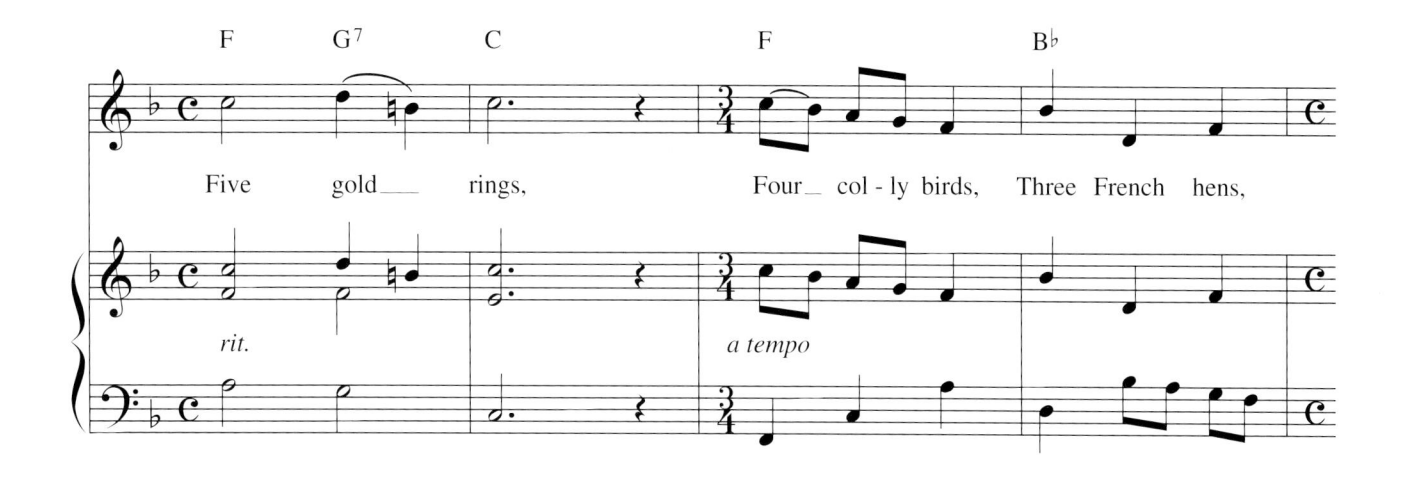

A Riddle and a Song

Now that you've nearly reached the end of this book (and I hope you've been singing along), I'd like to ask you a riddle: What present is given to you which you can never keep for yourself? You can keep books and puzzles, although I expect you will allow your friends to read the books and play with the games. You *can* also keep a whole box of chocolates, but I'm sure you're the sort of person who would share them. So what present *can't* you keep for yourself? Have you guessed the answer yet?

The answer is LOVE.

Love is for sharing. If your mum or dad gives you a hug before you set off for school, it makes you FEEL happy and so you LOOK happy, and the people you meet can tell you're in a good mood. You smile at your teacher and that puts him or her in a good mood. (Try it!) So the lesson goes well, and all through the day the hug that meant that your mum and dad love you has gone round in a circle. There's a saying 'It's love that makes the world go round', and it really is true.

The birds see much more of our world than we do. In the early morning you can hear them singing a special song called the Dawn Chorus. This same song is being sung every minute of the day and night, all around the world. As our world moves around the sun, it is always morning *somewhere*, and so the world is forever filled with bird-song. I think this turns it into a carousel, an endlessly moving roundabout where there is always beautiful music.

Carousel

Introduction:

1. This world of ours is a
2. Machines and computers may

ca - rou - sel, The birds know the music and sing it so well. But
have their place, But we've let them obscure the world's natural face. So

man's lost his rhythm and man's out of tune, In his race into space he's lost
let's take time to stand and stare, The joy that we seek is al-

E E7 A A7 D B7/D♯
sight of the moon, and the sun and the stars and the flow'rs and the trees,
read - y there. If you stand in a mea - dow or wait in a wood, The
1.
A/E E7 A
On - ly the birds know the world's made of these.
2.
A/E
rhy - thm of life will
E7 A E Bm7 E A Bm7 C♯m7
be un - der - stood. For the bird - song we hear is a cease - less song, An
F♯m7 F♯m7/E D♯m7♭5 E D A/C♯
end - less dawn cho - rus our whole lives long. From morn till dusk and the

Although, for purposes of demonstration, the song has been recorded electronically, it has been orchestrated for flutes, harp and percussion (with added bird-song).

Carousel

This world of ours is a carousel,
The birds know the music and sing it so well.
But man's lost his rhythm and man's out of tune,
In his race into space he's lost sight of the moon
And the sun and stars and the flowers and the trees,
Only the birds know the world's made of these.

Machines and computers may have their place,
But we've let them obscure the world's natural face.
So let's take time to stand and stare,
The joy that we seek is already there.
If you stand in a meadow or wait in a wood,
The rhythm of life will be understood.

For the bird-song we hear is a ceaseless song,
An endless dawn chorus our whole lives long.
From morn till dusk and the whole night through,
Somewhere in the world dawn is breaking anew.
And the birds sing their message and constantly call
That the Earth's survival depends on us all.